Today We
Became
Engaged

Written by
DIANNE AHERN

Illustrated by
KATHERINE LARSON

Published by Aunt Dee's Attic
A Division of Élan Systems

A BOOK FROM AUNT DEE'S ATTIC

Published by Élan Systems, Inc.
415 Detroit Street, Suite 200
Ann Arbor, MI 48104

Printed and bound in Canada

Library of Congress Control Number:2001118333

ISBN 0-9679437-1-X

1 2 3 4 5 6 7 8 9 10

First Edition

www.auntdeesattic.com

ACKNOWLEDGEMENTS

To the people whose stories are profiled in this book, I say *Thank you*. To my friends and family members who have made a commitment to making your marriages work, my hat is off to you. I proudly use your names and lessons in this special book. Thank you also to Cokie and Steve Roberts for the use of their story (*From This Day Forward,* William Morrow Co., 2000) and to William Bennett (*The Book of Virtues,* Simon & Schuster, 1993) for allowing me to quote from his book. To friends and family members who haven't quite found the formula for successful marriage, my heart goes out to you. Please keep trying. I use your stories so that others might learn from your ill-fate, but I will not reveal your real names.

How many writers are fortunate enough to have a friend who is also their spiritual advisor and is a former teacher of English writing to review and comment on their book manuscript? I extend a special thank you to Father Roger Prokop, Pastor of St. Thomas the Apostle Catholic Church in Ann Arbor for finding the time to work with me on this book. I am also indebted to Kristin Bos and Barbara Kelly for their expert review and editorial assistance.

Other individuals who provided review, commentary, and advice for which I am forever grateful and to whom I owe a big thank you are Linda Ahern, JoAnn Catalfio, Leo DiGiulio, Thomas Loewe, and Michelle Miner.

The inspiration for many of Katherine Larson's illustrations is the Fernwood Botanic Garden and Nature Center in Niles, Michigan. A special thanks to the Fernwood Center's staff and to the Dexter School of Dance for coordinating models for Katherine's illustrations. Thanks to schoolmates Zeke Allen Duke, Amanda C. Geisser, Andrew J. Jurgensen, Austin C. Psychas, Claire Shea, Jenna B. Spiner, and Daniel S. Stefanski, and to our good friends Kristin Bos and Josiah Shurtliff, for your poise and patience. Not to be forgotten are Angel and Elsa, best four-legged friends of the author and illustrator, respectively.

DEDICATION

*This book is dedicated to
my parents,
Mary and Vernon Ahern.*

*May the values
they gave their children
be passed on to their children
and their children's children.*

CONTENTS

Congratulations!

You Are Engaged To Be Married!

Something magical happens when two people decide they want to spend the rest of their lives together. They go from being boyfriend and girlfriend to the threshold of being totally committed to one another for as long as they both shall live, regardless of health or wealth. It is the time to revel in the mystery of what lies ahead – soon a wedding and a honeymoon, then a home, children, mingling of families and friends, sharing joys, sharing sorrows, and most importantly, the two becoming one through marriage.

The betrothal or engagement period should be cherished as that special time for a man and woman to meld their goals and values, to prepare a home to be shared, and to make the transition from single life to married life. It is also a time for each to look deep into his or her heart and discern that marriage is truly a calling freely accepted and that the future spouse is not only a best friend but will forever be a *soul mate.*

Why You and Me?

Love, Attraction, Differences, and Attachment

Today you are an authority on love. Love may even be consuming your every thought and breath. There is something inside you; maybe it's near where you think your heart should be that says I want to be so close to you that I want to breathe for you. I love you so deeply that I want to become one with you. I want to be married to you.

If you can think at all, you might be asking yourselves – Where does this feeling of love come from? Why did we fall in love with each other? If we are so in love, why don't we always see things the same? Will our love last forever? What will happen when we get old?

Let's explore!

What Is Love and Where Does It Come From?

We are taught from a very early age that human beings are a unique combination of body and soul. It is not surprising then to realize that love is part of this body-soul experience.

The body side of the combination is easy for us to understand. The body is us – we can see it and we can feel it, inside and out. Our body tells us we are hungry and we eat; we are cold and we put on a coat; we read a book and learn something new; we hear a bird sing and enjoy the sound. Biologists and doctors tell us we have genes and hormones that make each of us unique from the moment of our conception. Many of the things in life that we admire, like, or say that we love, are the result of our everyday experience. That is the body side.

The soul side is a little trickier to understand, but hopefully some examples will help. The story of *Genesis* tells us that God made man, all the plants and animals, and He made woman (again, this is the body side). Then God breathed life into all He had created, and He endowed different creatures with different abilities and powers – this is the soul side. Among the powers God gave man and woman is the *power to love*. Through the mystery of conception and birth, God gives each human being the *power to love*. This *power to love* resides in the soul of man and woman.

You might ask, If God gave us all the *power to love*, why aren't all people loving (and some seem downright hateful!)? Recall again the story of

Genesis. God not only gave man and woman the power to love, but he also gave them a free will – the *ability* to choose between right and wrong, between good and evil, between this or that, etc. Therefore our *ability* to use the *power of love* is affected throughout life by our free will choices, as well as our human or body experiences.

A parent says to their first-born, "You must love the new baby because he is your brother." The older child's understanding of love and ability to love is thus stimulated. The child knows Mommy and Daddy love him/her, and instinctively (perhaps through that mystery of the *power of love*) the child loves them back. Now the older child recognizes that he/she is to love this new baby too. That *power to love* is there, it just needs to be stimulated and directed to the new baby.

A tourist looks at a beautiful picture hanging in a museum and says, "I love this piece." The work of art created by another human being expands her concept of love and the emotions associated with love. The eyes see the beauty; the heart and soul feel the love.

For the first time, an adolescent boy holds a young girl's hand because he wants to, and begins to recognize what adult love might feel like. Sure it may be hormones that are triggering the reaction, but the emotion felt might be the very beginnings of something more than mere biology: namely, the ability to care deeply for another human being.

You are kissed on the lips and get a tingle from head to toe, and your breath escapes. You want to share this overwhelming emotion and kiss the other person back. The bells and whistles go off in your head and you know instinctively that this is *love*. The physical contact awoke that *power to love* and an overwhelming body and soul reaction just happened.

But how do we know the tingle from the kiss is love as opposed to hormonal reaction and sexual attractiveness? Is it possible to be physically attracted to a person without being in love or even really liking who that person is? Absolutely! Most of us realize that from adolescence on, there is a constant battle raging within us over sexual attractiveness and real love. It is definitely confusing, but it is essential to discern the difference before getting married. Perhaps the test that love exists may be when you have the same tingle deep inside your heart by just being with the other person as best friends, without physical contact.

Today you look into the eyes of your fiancé/fiancée and say and feel, "I love you and because I care for you so much, I want to spend the rest of my life with you." The body and soul experiences of your life so far make you realize that you have the ability to love another with your entire being for a lifetime.

Soon you will stand side-by-side to be married and will commit to creating a life of love together – together body and soul.

Why Are We Attracted To Each Other?

Psychologists, anthropologists, sociologists, and endocrinologists have spent centuries studying the differences between men and women in order to figure out why we choose the mates we do. Suffice it to say selection may include:

- Cupid's arrow
- Fate
- Divine intervention
- Hormones and other body chemistry
- Being at the right place at the right time

From the day we are born, and even while we are in the womb, we start developing likes and dislikes that affect us our entire lives. We are attracted to people and things that make us feel happy, comfortable, safe, and loved; that are appealing to our eyes, and are pleasing to our palates. As we mature, our likes and dislikes progress from taste, sound, and touch, to include the way people talk, the way others dress, the stories they tell, etc. Our selection of friends and *soul mates* is greatly influenced by these very early experiences and attractions.

My father was a farmer. He was a wonderful, kind, intelligent, nurturing human being. I remember from early childhood that on Sundays and other special days he always wore a crisp white shirt, fashionable suit, and tie. He looked so handsome in his suit, with his tanned face and hands, that I wished for more special days so he would dress-up more often. To this day, I am attracted to handsome men dressed in business suits with white shirts and ties.

Our programming toward the eventual selection of a mate matures as we mature. Along about the age of ten or twelve, the opposite sex stops being "yucky," and starts to become interesting. There is no doubt that this change is strongly influenced by changes in body chemistry and hormones. It is no surprise then, that at this age, our likes and dislikes, what we find attractive and unattractive, begin to focus on such things as physical attributes, grooming habits, manners, and charm.

By the teenage years the adult hormones really kick-in, and boys and girls develop a deeper curiosity about the opposite sex and stronger feelings about what is attractive and what is not. Suddenly it is not only what we find attractive that matters, but now we want to make ourselves more attractive to others – to them, that opposite sex, that future mate. We want to be "cool," to dress fashionably, be well groomed, smell good, have good manners, go to the right places, etc.

So that
others
notice us. So that
others are attracted to us. So that
we become attractive to them.

It is somewhere between the teens
and eternity, that our attractiveness
likes/dislikes mature from feeling and
appearance-based to include *value-based* likes
and dislikes. We observe and care about how someone
treats his/her friends, parents, and even pets. We may
admire honesty and forthrightness in others. We notice
if they are tolerant of people of different race or religious
belief. Then we compare their behavior to our values and
decide whom we like and whom we don't like.

My friend Tammy thinks a man's eyes, smile, and
sense of humor are the most important criteria for
selecting a lifelong mate. On the other hand, my
sister Barbara has always been attracted to
intelligent, creative, devout men, who share her
fondness for detective novels; she considers
looks secondary. Tammy has been married
twice and is on the verge of her second divorce.
Barbara and her husband, Tom, will soon be
celebrating 40 years of marriage. I observe
that Tammy places a lot of emphasis on

appearances when selecting partners and hasn't yet learned
to focus on *values*. Barbara and Tom, on the other hand, are
very together in their values and secure in their marriage.

These *value-based* likes and dislikes are influenced not only
by family and friends, but also through
involvement in education, religion, work,
and co-workers. Our values are what make
us who we are. As adults, we enrich our
lives by knowing and making friends with all
kinds of people. But when thinking about
a mate, it is often his/her values that are
most important.

Now, there is one additional
attractiveness factor that brings two
people together as marriage partners;
that is, the *intense desire to care for
one another*. True marriage partners
are so deeply concerned about the
welfare of each other that they will
take whatever actions necessary to
ensure the other's well being and
happiness. In fact, these *soul mates*
are so concerned about the welfare of
each other that they are willing to
enter into an irreversible life-long
commitment to live together and
love each other exclusively as
husband and wife.

Why Do We See Things So Differently Sometimes?

A physician friend once told me, "Men and women are so different, it is hard to imagine they belong to the same species." Amen! And aren't we glad about that?!

Men and women are definitely attracted to each other, but they are attracted in different ways. As the saying goes: *A woman looks at a man and thinks about what it would be like to spend the rest of her life with him. A man looks at a woman and wonders what it would be like to spend the rest of the night with her.*

Men and women do look at each other differently because they are different. A woman's instinct says she wants to know a relationship with a man will be long term before getting seriously involved and certainly before making a commitment to marry. This instinct probably comes from the

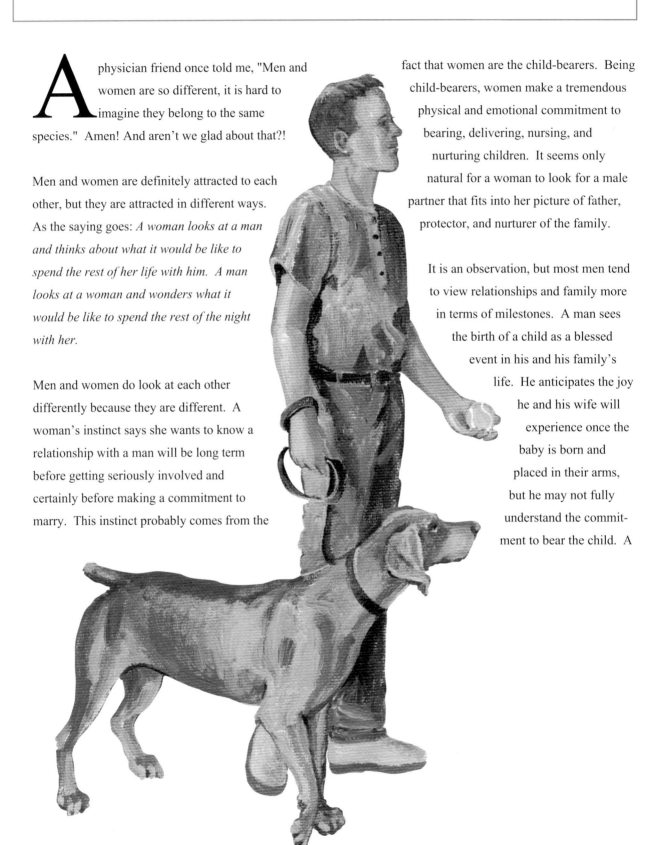

fact that women are the child-bearers. Being child-bearers, women make a tremendous physical and emotional commitment to bearing, delivering, nursing, and nurturing children. It seems only natural for a woman to look for a male partner that fits into her picture of father, protector, and nurturer of the family.

It is an observation, but most men tend to view relationships and family more in terms of milestones. A man sees the birth of a child as a blessed event in his and his family's life. He anticipates the joy he and his wife will experience once the baby is born and placed in their arms, but he may not fully understand the commitment to bear the child. A man's instinct is to be the protector, the provider and head of the family, responsible for hearth and home.

Have you noticed that couples gain a great deal of happiness and satisfaction out of doing things together, but they actually experience things differently while doing them? For instance, some men and women enjoy going to automobile races together, but his focus is on the performance of the race cars while she is more fascinated with people-watching. Couples go to the hardware store together; while he analyzes the difference between stainless steel and galvanized bolts, she goes to the housewares section and looks for things to make their home more attractive. They watch a movie together and there is a scene that makes her cry. He is not sure why she is crying, but wants to hug her, assure her that everything is all right, and promises to try to prevent from happening in real life what made her sad in the movie.

Conversations among spouses and friends also highlight big differences between men and women. Husbands and wives do have conversations that are extremely intimate, intense, and meaningful which focus on their lives together, their values, and solving home-related problems. And that is good! And that is essential! However, if a woman wants a good "gab session," she better call her sister or best girlfriend because, although he will listen, he does not necessarily know how to "talk the talk." If he wants to talk about the satisfaction of repairing his motorcycle, he better call his buddy rather than his wife. She might listen, but probably won't fully appreciate the accomplishment.

How Do We Know That We Will Always Be In Love?

At a recent 25th anniversary celebration, I was touched by Matt's toast to Irene. "Being in love with you and being married to you is just so comfortable, and it just gets better year after year!"

There are no guarantees in life, and therefore no guarantee that you will love each other forever. However, as an observer of couples, I become increasingly aware that the more each person puts into a relationship, the more likely the friendship and love will not only last a lifetime, but will grow and intensify over time.

Investing *more than 100%* in respect, kindness, understanding, and shared values is essential – for both husband and wife. *Caution!* If you don't feel you can make a 100% investment in caring for your mate, then stop now! Do not become engaged; do not think of marriage. However, if you both want to make the investment, and are actually excited about it, you have the foundation for a lifetime of joy.

You will learn in the coming years that there is an incredible bond that develops between two people who spend their lives together. That bond is called *attachment*. It comes from sleeping together in the same bed night after night, sitting across from each other at the dinner table day after day, grieving lost loved ones together, celebrating victories together, having intimate moments together. An intimate moment may be sex in the afternoon when you are sixty, or it may be looking each other in the eye during a boring movie and knowing, without saying a word, that you both want to leave, NOW. *Attachment* is what happens when the raging hormones of our youth mature. It is love. Love from the body and soul.

The following poem, *The Human Touch*, by Spincer Michael Free, comes from *The Book of Virtues* by William Bennett (Simon & Schuster, 1993), and speaks of the closeness of hands, hearts, and souls. It speaks of *attachment.*

> *'Tis the human touch in this world that counts,*
> *The touch of your hand in mine,*
> *Which means far more to the fainting heart*
> *Than shelter and bread and wine;*
> *For shelter is gone when the night is o'er,*
> *And bread lasts only a day,*
> *But the touch of the hand and the sound of the voice*
> *Sing on in the soul alway.*

Shared Values
That Will Make Our Lives One

THE FUTURE TOGETHER

Everyone has advice for you on how to make your marriage last. Couples we asked who have lasting and loving relationships frequently said having a sense of humor and knowing how to lighten-up are very important ingredients for a good marriage. Others cited trust, open communications, religion, and being best friends as key elements.

My best friends Joanne and Dick Hill knew they were soul mates from their very first date. Their advice: "trusting each other is important, but so is being willing to tolerate a little foolishness now and then." Joanne and Dick eloped 30 years ago and today are absolutely sure they have another thirty years left on their original contract.

My parents had a very healthy and happy marriage. They made it look so easy and I wish now that I had asked them their secret. I think they might have said their faith and desire to pray together. Each evening before bed the house would be made quiet and the entire family would kneel and pray together. You know it is nearly impossible to go to bed mad, angry, or upset after you pray.

Belief in God, having a clear sense of moral and family values, and practicing one's faith has kept couples like Heber and Eunice Barnard together for over 50 years. Through a lifetime of joys and sorrows, successes and disappointments, she can still say, "He is just really fun to have around!"

Opposites may attract, but they do not always achieve that bond of *attachment*. Happily married couples insist that it is important to share common values throughout married life. Among the most important values for married couples to share are *commitment, fairness, courage, compassion, honesty, respect,* and *forgiveness.*

COMMITMENT

Commitment means making a pledge or promise to pour one's energies and resources into succeeding at one's goals. A commitment to a *marriage vow* is promising to *love and honor each other. . . with your whole heart and soul . . . until death do you part.* It is probably the biggest commitment you will ever make. However, this huge commitment implicates an entire lifetime of other commitments.

Married couples clearly have personal commitments to each other through their marriage vows. But through matrimony the two become one in a new psychological and spiritual reality. This new union has its own commitments to family, friends, community, and God.

A marriage creates a new family, but it does not, cannot, should not sever the bonds between the new bride and groom and their existing family members. A commitment to family (including the in-law family) may take a good deal of energy, especially if the families are of different socioeconomic backgrounds, race, culture, or continents. My nephew, Bob, married a wonderful woman, Fazila, whose family lives on an island, Mauritius, on the other side of the world from us. Fazila and Bob made a commitment to keep a strong sense of family in their marriage. They literally travel to the ends of the earth (children in tow) to make this happen. The strength of their marriage and commitment to family has blessed us all.

Friends are almost as important as family in sustaining healthy marriages. A couple brings together two sets of friends and then builds a new set of couple friends. The added responsibilities of marriage, family, in-laws, and home often cause couples to rearrange the way they spend their time. Unfortunately, the easiest place to find the extra time needed to deal with added responsibilities is to take it away from time otherwise spent with old friends. Once married, daily contact may no longer be practical, but committing periodically to picking up the telephone to hear how old friends are doing or setting aside special days or weekends to get together is fun and beneficial for all.

Being part of a community also means committing to its well-being. As a married couple you may be asked to give to your community and church through service, volunteerism, mentoring, etc. Often one hears that young couples "get married and settle down." In reality they get married and, because they are concerned about the kind of world in which they and their future children will live, they take a proactive role to ensure the well-being of their community and society.

So many people I interviewed for this book cited a commitment to their church and religious beliefs as essential ingredients to a successful marriage. Faith in God and the practice of one's religious beliefs ranked very high among the qualities that mates admire most in their spouses. Throughout life there are many temptations, tests of strength, and tragedies that require a strong faith in God to help marriages endure and survive. Likewise, there are untold times of absolute joy that are recognized as God's work that couples celebrate together.

FAIRNESS

Fairness in life is putting self-interest, bias, and prejudice aside and holding the same standards for everyone. It is following the Golden Rule: *Treat others as you want to be treated, and do unto others as you would have others do unto you.*

In a marriage, fairness is not taking advantage of your mate. It is calling your spouse if you'll be home late, explaining why, and saying where you'll be if he/she needs to get in touch with you. It's listening when your spouse has something to say or share. Being fair is respecting the right of your spouse to have opinions, to think and speak freely, and to make the best use of his/her abilities.

Many an unhappy marriage results from one partner feeling he/she has to dominate the other and withholds conversation, companionship, and affection. This domination often manifests itself in psychological, verbal, and physical abuse. This kind of behavior is not fair and prevents a marriage from being fulfilled.

Fairness is also making time for others to come into your lives. My friends Jacqueline and Michael are lucky (and some may say not so lucky) to have both sets of parents living within ten miles of them. Holidays and other special days can become quite a juggling act, trying to fit in time to see everyone. But they understand the tremendous value grandparents and other family members have in the lives of their children and the absolute importance of family togetherness. It is only fair to make time for everyone.

COURAGE

Courage is the willingness to commit to a goal that others may say is impossible, but that is important to the two of you. Courage gives us strength to be honest about our emotions, our faith, and our practices. Courage is what keeps us moving in the right direction without deviation caused by fear or temptation.

In their book, *From This Day Forward* (William Morrow Co., 2000), Cokie and Steve Roberts describe what I consider a very courageous step in planning their lives together. Cokie is Catholic and Steve is Jewish. They recognized that their individual embrace of religion was part of who they are and what attracted them to each other in the first place. As they began planning their marriage, Cokie and Steve made a commitment not only to maintain their respective religious beliefs but to make the observance of solemn customs and traditions a priority. Many wise people thought Cokie and Steve were crazy, but they had the courage to commit and to make it work.

It takes courage just to examine and affirm one's own convictions, let alone delve into another's. Today there is an increasing number of so-called mixed marriages of couples who have different religious beliefs as well as different cultural and racial backgrounds. It is scary to delve deeply into another's culture or belief, mostly for fear that we may uncover something to make us want to change our minds (and God knows how afraid we all are of change). But, if you are in this group, you must become a student of each other's basic nature and culture. Embrace the knowledge, respect your differences, and face the world together.

Courage is also being able to admit to and then deal with one's shortcomings, weaknesses, and mistakes. No one is perfect. Everyone makes mistakes. It takes courage to admit to mistakes and accept responsibility for righting a wrong. It also takes courage to ask for forgiveness and even more courage to forgive. How many marriages are ruined because of lack of courage to say, *"I am sorry!?"*

COMPASSION

When God revealed himself to Moses at Mount Sinai, He delivered to Moses and to all humanity His Commandments. Some 1200 to 1300 years later, Jesus Christ spoke to his Apostles about the most important Commandment:

To love the Lord our God with all our hearts, souls, minds, and strength, and to love our neighbors as ourselves

From the time of Moses, to the time of Christ, now and always, God instructs us to act with compassion.

Most of us know within ourselves the emotions of love, sorrow, pain, pride, joy, and happiness. What we find difficult, however, is sharing these emotions with another person. What is even more difficult is to put ourselves in another's shoes and try to understand how that person feels these emotions.

In marriage you must love your spouse as yourself to achieve that oneness of being. Together you must love your children, to whom you give life, your parents, who gave you life, and your community, of which you are a part.

I have an acquaintance I'll call Bridgett. Bridgett happens to be married to one of my best friends, Sam. Bridgett was raised by an adoring aunt and grandmother after her mother became ill and her father abandoned them. Somewhere along the way Bridgett became a very bitter and selfish person. Bridgett's entire life today is centered around building "security" for herself through accumulation of material possessions and money. She ignores her old friends and speaks with contempt of people who try to befriend her. She is incapable of nurturing her husband and their children.

Many who know her feel a great deal of compassion for Bridgett because she can neither feel nor give love right now. Unfortunately, their marriage may not survive unless Bridgett can find compassion within herself; she must find a way to love herself, her husband, their children, and friends.

Having compassion for others provides a better life for you and helps you to do the right thing. For instance, I observe Bridgett and I am inspired to love my family more and to do whatever I can to help her, Sam, and their children.

Acting compassionately not only feels right and good, but it has other rewards. Some very special couples see the neglected children of the world and reach out by becoming foster parents. Their rewards are the children's hugs and knowing they just might save a soul. I know a retired couple who volunteer weekly to prepare meals for the homeless. At the end of that day they go home exhausted but happily confess, "it just feels so good to know that you helped those in need."

Perhaps you have friends who are a little stressed and in need of a night out. Volunteer to keep their children while they take in a movie and dinner. You will have fun with the children, and the couple will enjoy being adults without child-care responsibilities for a whole evening. What a respite for them!

In the future you might see your partner struggling with a problem at work. Give him or her a little extra space to work it out and you may be amazed at how his/her love and respect for you is multiplied in return. That's practicing compassion. It's loving your neighbor as yourself. It makes a marriage rich!

HONESTY

Honesty is living life in truth. Sounds easy, right? Well, did you ever notice that honesty is one of the most difficult of all virtues to master?

Take an ordinary day and write down the number of dishonest occasions, untruths, and outright lies you witness. Does your list look like this?

- Told someone you liked her dress, but really didn't
- Let the answering machine pick-up because you didn't want to let someone know you were home
- Gave a vendor an advantage over a competitor because you liked him better
- Twisted the truth to gain an advantage or appear more popular
- Withheld information that someone asked for
- Made a promise you had no intention of keeping
- Said "I'm fine, thank you" when really your feelings were hurt
- Pretended you had something in your eye when you were actually crying

Some things on this list may seem funny and trivial. However, if being dishonest harms someone else or makes someone else view another person with disrespect, it is wrong.

In marriage, in what should be the most intimate and honest bond between two people, dishonesty often manifests itself. This dishonesty left to grow will kill a marriage.

- The proverbial "Not tonight, I have a headache"
- Saying, "You go rest, dear, and I'll take the garbage out" (but have no intention of doing so)
- Telling a spouse you have to work over the weekend, when in fact you are spending time with someone else
- Secretly taking money out of the house account to gamble or buy drugs
- Having your spouse call your boss and lie about your being sick

Today, by becoming engaged, you are agreeing that some day soon you will stand before each other and *vow* to *love and honor* each other *until death do you part*. Implicit in the vow of marriage is to live together in truth and honesty.

How do we cultivate honesty in our lives and our relationships if it's not there now? *Practice, practice, practice.* See how much fun the two of you can have being completely honest and always telling the truth. Honesty is a great turn-on, and a great step toward intimacy. Honesty can create a bond between two people that nobody or nothing can break.

RESPECT

Friendship, betrothal, and marriage require that a partnership (not a possession!) exist between two people. In order for the partnership to exist, there must be mutual respect and regard for one another.

Respect is giving the one you love the room to grow as an individual with the full understanding that allowing your partner to be his or her own person allows your union to be as one.

Without respect, the ability to love and be loved is missing. Selfishness and jealousy in a marriage are indications that one regards the other as a possession – and you cannot possess another person! Without respect, marriages fail.

I have a friend, Alice, who at age forty, wanted desperately to go back to school and complete her teaching degree. She convinced her husband, Ted, she could do it by taking night classes, even if it meant driving 110 miles round trip to the nearest university three nights a week. Ted said, "Fine. If that's what you want, go for it. I will support your decision." Eight weeks into the program, Alice seemed like one of the happiest people on earth. She had good grades, felt intellectually challenged, and saw one of her dreams was actually going to come true. And she was extremely grateful to Ted for allowing her this opportunity. However, Ted soon started to complain about her not being home at night, studying all the time, not keeping up with her housework, and acting like a "smart college kid." Ted started going out to the bars the nights she was in school, and even started staying away on nights she was home. Ted was obviously very jealous of Alice's school interest and wanted the comfort and attention she once gave him. Alice could not accept that what she was doing was hurting Ted and their marriage and criticized his "childish" behavior. Unfortunately for them and their children, it was easier to divorce than to put aside their jealousies and selfishness and try to rebuild the respect they once had for each other.

Respect doesn't begin with marriage. For you, the engaged couple, it begins now, especially with regard to lifestyles and things important to each of you. A lifestyle issue that often comes up before marriage is the issue of premarital sex and cohabitation. Often couples or maybe only one partner wishes to wait until after marriage to have sex and/or live together.

Whether this desire is based on personal preference or religious traditions, it must be respected. Being soul mates first, having a relationship steeped in mutual trust, honesty, commitment, respect, and fairness, will guarantee that life together and sex will be totally fulfilling and consuming in the marriage covenant. The opposite is not true. That two people can have "great sex" is no indication that they will ever become *soul mates*.

While we are on the subject, and whether you agree or not, you should know that sociological studies have proved, absolutely (by statistics), that couples who hold off on cohabitation and sexual activity are much more likely to remain married to each other than couples who do not. Why? One theory is that sexual involvement is sufficiently compelling as to "blind" people to qualities they don't really like in their partner. After marriage, when sexual excitement may lessen, those unnoticed qualities become woefully apparent. Another theory is that cohabitation during the engagement period makes saying, "No, this isn't right for me," very difficult. After all, if you and your intended are paying bills together, buying food together, and sleeping together, the whole momentum of your current existence makes it hard to pull away, if, in fact, that is what you need to do. As an engaged couple, you owe it to yourselves to look at your options openly and honestly – and with a conscience. And remember: the engagement period is a time for discernment, for making sure.

Respect is doing for each other what is in the best interest of the other person, even if it compromises your desires. Respect is keeping yourself well groomed and healthy. Respect is allowing your partner to have an opinion that is different from yours. Respect is siding with your spouse when the in-laws want to insert their opinions in your lives. Respect is being there for your partner when you want to be somewhere else. Respect costs nothing, but conveys everything. Respect is saying, *I want to please you, because pleasing you pleases me.*

Remember, marriage is not a 50-50 deal; it's 100 percent commitment from each of you!

FORGIVENESS

Every child is taught the saying by Alexander Pope: *To err is human, to forgive divine.* It is so important to practice this in our daily lives.

Forgiveness grows out of the recognition that making mistakes and being insensitive are a part of life, and we are all guilty. Forgiveness requires two parties and two distinct sets of action. First, the person who failed must be remorseful about the wrongdoing and truly want the other person to forgive him/her. Secondly, the person who was wronged must not only be willing to grant a pardon, but must do so without harboring resentment.

All couples have their run-ins, and this one about Leo and Anna demonstrates the blessing of forgiveness. They had just moved into their new home and Anna wanted to be the perfect homemaker and gardener. They had a small greenhouse and she decided to put it to use by growing her own bedding plants. Anna started with seeds in February and by late April she had a greenhouse full of healthy plants ready for transplant. She was rightfully proud. Then one day Leo went into the greenhouse and forgot to close the door on his way out. It wasn't long before the rabbits discovered the plants and ate off all the foliage. Anna was furious; she called Leo all kinds of names – careless klutz, irresponsible imbecile, and numbskull, just to name a few. He tried to apologize, but Anna would have none of it. That night it was a can of soup for dinner and the couch for a bed. The next morning Anna's place at the breakfast table was set with the good china, a vase of cut flowers, and a homemade card. The card had a picture of a rabbit with Leo's face pasted on it and a big "I'm sorry" underneath. Anna realized how petty she was to get so upset over what happened. After all, it wasn't intentional, the plants could be replaced, and she had already had months of pleasure from greenhouse gardening. She forgave Leo his carelessness and he forgave her callousness and promised to try harder; they were happy once again. Best of all, those chewed-off plants grew back and gave them beautiful flowers all summer long, not to mention a lifetime of happy memories.

In a marriage, you trust that each is doing his/her best and is looking out for the best interests of the other. However, sooner or later, each of you will almost for sure make a mistake that will challenge the relationship and threaten the trust you have in each other. The act needing forgiveness may be as small as being late for a date. It may be a medium-sized error, like forgetting a birthday or wedding anniversary. God forbid, it's that most humongous mistake of all, marital infidelity.

Think about how you will deal with each other's mistakes, the little ones, medium-sized ones, and the big one. Will you be able to forgive and forget? Will you be willing to say you are sorry, promise never to do it again, and keep the promise? Will your partner be able to trust you to keep your promise? Forgiveness requires and sends a powerful message of trust. By accepting forgiveness, you must live up to your spouse's expectation, recognize the problem, and commit to changing.

Earlier I mentioned my friend Tammy who has been married twice and is on the verge of another divorce. Tammy recently discovered that her husband has had a three-year relationship with another woman. Although Jack ended the relationship and promised never, ever to get involved with another woman, Tammy is not sure she can forgive him. She sincerely believes Jack will never again have an extramarital affair. He sees the damage that has been done and is truly remorseful. Tammy thinks that if it were a "one-night-stand" she could forgive him and they could get on with their lives. However, the duration of Jack's infidelity and his apparent lack of respect for their marriage vows may be more than Tammy can ever forgive. What would you do?

History
OF BETROTHAL AND ENGAGEMENT

There are many traditions and customs surrounding engagements and weddings that are observed by families, cultures, and religions. Some of these customs can be traced back thousands and thousands of years. The connection between past and present can provide some interesting insights into the engagement rite.

Betrothal Versus Engagement

We sometimes hear couples refer to one another as his or her betrothed. It sounds charming, but is it accurate?

Betrothal is defined as the *giving of one's troth –* that is giving one's true promise of a future marriage. It is a solemn promise, not merely an intention, entered into freely by two parties. The promise given is mutual and is true, sincere, and given by both parties with the intention of binding oneself to another.

Engagement is a term commonly used today to describe the time between when a couple agrees to marry and when they actually get married. It is defined as a promise, agreement, or commitment to be in a specific place at a specific time for a specified purpose, i.e., marriage.

The major difference between *betrothal* and *engagement* is the level of the commitment. Betrothal infers a solemn commitment or vow. Engagement is a promise, something less than a vow. Note that promises can be broken, vows should never be broken.

In the recorded history of Israel, more than 4,000 years ago, the custom was that couples became betrothed first, planned their wedding, then got married. Today, couples become engaged, plan their wedding, and the betrothal, i.e., *to plight one's troth*, is part of the marriage ceremony.

Interestingly, the very early Jewish laws were based in great measure on the supposition that a marriage meant the purchase of a wife for the man. Virgins were betrothed by their fathers to future husbands based on a purchase price. The woman had little input on the selection, and love and compatibility were not considered important, unless of course she had an understanding father.

By the time of Moses (13th century B.C.), Hebrew law began referring to contracts of betrothal or promises of marriage between the man and woman (rather than between the man/groom and the woman's father). However, the practice of paying for the bride continued for some time. It wasn't until much later, under the influence of Roman law (which was after the birth of Christ), that the concept of "buying" a wife was abolished. (NOTE: We observe that in some non Judeo-Christian cultures, the practice of arranged marriages still exists.)

It was as recently as the fourteenth century A.D., that religious leaders began to oppose the concept of betrothal as a binding contract. Betrothals became more a time of discernment with a promise to be married, i.e., an engagement that could be broken should either party want out. However, the actual wedding, wherein the couple did plight one's troth, was then and always has been considered a binding contract under both religious and public law.

Terms of Engagement

A question often asked is, *How long is a proper engagement?* Some books on etiquette suggest a year. This advice has roots in tradition, as we will discover, but is also a practical response. The real answer is, *as long as it takes to be absolutely sure of the commitment and to prepare for the wedding and married life!*

In the ancient Hebrew tradition the betrothal period was usually twelve months. According to custom, the prospective bridegroom would take the initiative and travel to the home of his prospective wife. There he would negotiate with her father and they would agree on a price that must be paid to secure the man's daughter as a bride. Once paid, a marriage covenant or betrothal was said to have been established. At this point the man and woman would separate for a period of twelve months.

During this time, the man returned to his father's house and learned a trade to support his promised wife and their eventual family. The woman spent the time gathering wardrobe and housewares in order to set up a home for her bridegroom. At the end of the year, the bridegroom would return for his bride accompanied by other males carrying torches (these were the groom's men). The groom would be received by his wife with her female attendants (i.e., the bride's maids). The couple and their attendants would then return to his father's house, where the wedding and a celebration took place. Late in the celebration, one that probably went on for several days, the bride and groom would take leave and enter into their bridal chamber. There they would have physical union for the first time and consummate their marriage.

Giving of Engagement Ring

As early as the 1st century A.D., some proposals of marriage were accompanied by the man sending the woman an iron betrothal ring. However, the tradition of making a gift of a ring from the man to the woman to signify their betrothal became more customary during the Byzantine era (5th and 6th centuries) when bronze and iron rings were in vogue.

By late Middle Ages (7th to 15th centuries A.D.), the gold and diamond engagement ring emerged as the symbol of betrothal among European royalty. Archduke Maximilian of Austria is said to have been the first man to present a diamond ring when he proposed to Mary of Burgundy in 1477.

During the Middle Ages, diamonds were thought to have magnetic powers that could hold couples together. Five centuries later, diamonds remain the number one choice of stones, symbolizing lasting love, strength, faith, virtue, and spirituality.

Giving of Gifts and Dowry

In the discussion of early Hebrew tradition, it appears that the man's family paid for the purchase of the wife and for the wedding celebration, contrary to contemporary standards.

It was under Roman law that marriage ceased to be considered a wife-purchase arrangement. Coincidentally, at this time the custom of exchanging gifts between the couple and their families became common practice. At some point, the gift from the bride's family was considered a dowry and was intended to cover the cost of the wedding celebration and setting up the household. The often-observed custom of the bride's family paying for the wedding reception is a throwback to the dowry.

It is interesting to correlate from the earlier historical account of betrothal, how the custom of giving gifts to an engaged couple began. The bride traditionally has had the responsibility for pulling together the items needed to make a home for herself and her groom. It is only natural that a betrothed woman's mother, aunts, and female friends would want to give her as gifts the items they found useful in their own homes. Today bridal showers are popular social events in which family and friends meet and bestow useful household and personal gifts on the engaged couple.

Announcement of Betrothal and Engagement

At the beginning of the 3rd century A.D., betrothal was recognized by common law as a valid and lawful contract that could be witnessed by either religious leaders or public officials. The espousals would be contracted in writing, the instrument signed by religious and/or government authority, and read publicly. These contracts once made were not to be broken.

The practice of publishing an announcement of a couple's betrothal and impending marriage was common practice. The names of the betrothed couple and their parents would be read aloud during public meetings and published in Church documents on consecutive weeks. This was called publishing the *Banns of Marriage*. The purpose was to prevent invalid and illicit marriages between couples who were related, already married persons, celibate clergy, or people otherwise not free to marry. Any persons knowing why the two could not enter into a valid marriage were requested to come forward and present the information. The practice of publishing the *Banns* was carried out in Catholic and Protestant churches into the middle and late 20th century, and is still practiced in some communities.

The practice of placing couples' engagement announcements in newspapers today is no doubt an outcome of publishing the *Banns of Marriage*. Although today's practice may be more for social reasons, it does provide a means for the public to scrutinize and respond to notices.

On Your Knees or On a Mountain Top

T H E   P R O P O S A L

A proposal of marriage is one of the most significant interpersonal acts between two people who are not yet married, but who are madly in love with each other.

Caution! A proposal of marriage and the giving of an engagement ring is not the solution to a stormy or not-quite-there relationship. Sometimes proposals are made/accepted just to get the other person off your case, because all your friends are getting married, you are afraid you will end up old and alone, or you don't want to hurt someone's feelings. *Do not* offer or accept a proposal of marriage unless you are ready. Living with someone you do not love is painful. Divorce is expensive and heartbreaking. The trauma of saying "no" today may last months. If you are not ready, the trauma of saying "yes" will last a lifetime.

Proposals of marriage are as unique and as special as the two people involved. Some proposals are modest, others flamboyant, many outrageous, but most mirror the playfulness and fun of the couple's courtship. Most often it is the man who does the proposing. However, since the sexual revolution of the 70-80s, a lot of proposals are made by women.

As couples tell of their proposal stories, you realize that the proposal usually takes on the characteristic of a theatrical performance. The lead character, usually the male, is also the writer, director, and producer of the performance as well as the leading man. The audience is the woman, his intended, and his leading lady. Her review of the performance will seal the fate of their future together.

Some proposal backdrops are mysteries that force the audience, i.e., the woman, to sort through clues to get to the proposal and find the ring. Some are adventures that involve trips to exotic places.

The risks some men take in setting up a proposal are surprising. I have a friend who proposed to his wife-to-be by putting a diamond ring in her glass of champagne for a New Year's toast. He was so worried that she would not see it and swallow it, that he almost flubbed his lines.

Sports venues are favorite proposal settings for many men. Picture the plane flying over the football stadium on a beautiful fall afternoon toting a banner that says, "Marry Me Martha!" That is something only a guy would design, direct, and produce.

Some more dramatic and endearing proposals involve the man on bended knee, looking into the eyes of his beloved, and saying those classic words, "Will you marry me?" *Be still my heart!*

Where there is a sense of family obligation, there is often a pre-proposal performance, one that involves the woman's family. It may be old-fashioned, but asking a father for his daughter's hand in marriage is a clincher. Often it is the father who is the nervous one in this act! He may or may not be surprised, but it pleases a future father-in-law to be so honored.

Following the performance, i.e., the proposal and acceptance, there is generally a joyous celebration. The cast party to celebrate the performance may be just the couple or it may include family and friends.

The Ultimate Shopping Experience

T H E   R I N G

A favorite saying in our house is, "we are going to do this once, and we are going to do it right." We may end up spending more on something than is probably necessary, but we have the ultimate satisfaction of knowing it's the best we can afford, meets or exceeds our expectations, and will last for as long as we intend it to last.

Selection of the engagement ring is the ultimate shopping experience. You do it once, you do it right, and it lasts forever.

My nephew Brian agonized for months over the ring for his intended, Sally. He wanted to surprise her. However, Brian was afraid Sally might not like the ring he chose, so he made sure the ring was returnable before he actually bought it. Now think about this. If Brian was unsure of what they both wanted for an engagement ring, was he really ready for the big step? And, if Sally did exchange the ring after he spent so much time on the selection, would she really be the partner for him?

Brian is very methodical. He studied diamonds, their shape, color, clarity, and carat weight. He also researched types of metals for the ring: gold, yellow gold, white gold, silver, and platinum. Then he listed options for the types of settings he thought he and Sally would like: solitaire, three stone, solitaire with baguettes or diamond chips, raised or embedded stone, etc. Finally, he decided on a price range he was comfortable with – in the range of one to two times his current monthly salary. Although Brian shopped the local chain jewelry stores and department stores, he ended up having their engagement ring custom crafted by a local jeweler/artisan (who assured Brian that Sally could indeed bring it back if she didn't like it). Needless to say, the ring is beautiful; it exceeded Brian's expectations, and is something he and Sally will cherish forever. It was his special gift to her.

Other couples, like Tim and his fiancée, Mary Beth, made the selection of the engagement ring a shared adventure. Tim and Mary Beth picked a sunny day right before Christmas to visit the only jeweler in their small town. Tim was prepared to spend what he considered to be a lot of money for the ring, but was he in for a surprise! When he saw the prices on some of the rings he became lightheaded, tight-chested, weak-kneed, and had to sit down.

Mary Beth kept her eye out for the right ring, rejecting the jeweler's recommendations tray after tray. Then she found it. Alas, it was confirmed. Tim knew Mary Beth was the perfect mate when she picked a ring that was simple yet elegant, a little non-traditional, and totally within his budget. A match that is certainly made in heaven. A special day and a ring they will treasure always.

Remember, there is absolutely no correlation between the size of the diamond and the success of the marriage. The ring is a symbol of never-ending love. Real love resides in you, body and soul.

My God, What Have We Done!
And, What Do We Do Now?

THE ACCEPTANCE

You have just made one of the most exhilarating decisions of your entire life. You have accepted a proposal to spend the rest of your life with just one person. With that person you will make a home, create and raise children, endure hardships (in sickness and in health), share paychecks, and a whole lot more. *HOORAY FOR YOU!!!* You cannot imagine what your life together will be like. However, what you do know is that you love each other and you want to be together forever, which makes starting on this very long and exciting mystery trip worth the ride.

In the next few months, you have to plan a wedding celebration: determine who you will invite to the celebration, decide how you are going to pay for everything, select bridesmaids and groomsmen, hire caterers, reserve sites for the ceremony and reception, pick out clothing, get better acquainted with your future in-laws, and on and on. Potentially thousands of details to work on together. Make it fun.

My Aunt Winifred once told me that planning a wedding is good practice for couples because it helps them to learn how to overcome obstacles together. That's good news. I have lost count of the number of couples I talked to who said they nearly broke off their engagement because of the tensions and disagreements that arose over planning their wedding. I have heard stories of perfectly wonderful people being driven to near violence under the anticipation that something would go wrong, that one or the other was not getting his/her way, or that so-and-so's kids are coming to the wedding and will ruin everything. On the bright side, I do not know of one couple who actually cancelled their wedding because of the planning. Aunt Winifred certainly was a smart lady.

Looking beyond the wedding and its celebration, there is a lifetime of loving, sharing, and problem-solving to enjoy.

The End of The Beginning

As you have learned by now, this book will not tell you how to plan your wedding. You will find hundreds, even thousands of books, magazines, websites, and consultants to help you plan and execute a beautiful wedding. But hopefully this book will help you plan your life together – before and after the wedding.

Beginning today, your period of engagement, a time of discernment and preparation, will have its serious moments, its stressful moments, its terrifying moments, its funny moments, and its absolutely joyous moments. Done right, it will complete your successful transition from two individuals into one couple joined in marriage.

Congratulations and God Bless You!

The Story of
How We Met
and Our
Engagement
Day

Our
Story

OUR STORY

How we met:

_____

_____

_____

_____

_____

_____

_____

Our courtship:

_____

_____

_____

_____

_____

_____

_____

_____

_____

_____

_____

_____

_____

_____

_____

_____

_____

When we knew we were in love – She says:

_____
_____
_____
_____
_____
_____
_____
_____
_____
_____
_____
_____
_____
_____
_____

When we knew we were in love – He says:

_____
_____
_____
_____
_____
_____
_____
_____
_____
_____
_____
_____
_____
_____
_____

OUR ENGAGEMENT RING

When and where we bought it:

_____
_____
_____
_____

Who picked it out?

_____
_____
_____
_____

Physical description:

_____
_____
_____
_____

Paste the receipt here!

THE PROPOSAL

Who proposed to whom?

_____

_____

_____

Where did it happen?

_____

_____

_____

_____

How did it happen?

_____

_____

_____

_____

_____

_____

_____

_____

_____

_____

_____

_____

_____

_____

THE ACCEPTANCE

What was your first reaction?

_____

_____

_____

_____

What were the first words you said?

_____

_____

_____

_____

Then what happened?

_____

_____

_____

_____

_____

_____

_____

_____

_____

_____

_____

_____

_____

THE CELEBRATION

Who was the first person(s) you told about your engagement and what was their reaction?

_____
_____
_____
_____
_____
_____

What did you do to celebrate?

_____
_____
_____
_____
_____
_____

What were your parents'/family's reaction? (Hers)

_____
_____
_____
_____
_____
_____

What were your parents'/family's reaction? (His)

_____
_____
_____
_____
_____
_____

What did your friends do and say?

_____

_____

_____

_____

_____

_____

_____

_____

_____

_____

_____

_____

_____

_____

_____

_____

_____

_____

_____

_____

_____

_____

_____

_____

_____

_____

_____

_____

_____

_____

Our Story

PROMISES TO EACH OTHER

He says:

_____

_____

_____

_____

_____

_____

_____

_____

_____

_____

_____

_____

She says:

_____

_____

_____

_____

_____

_____

_____

_____

_____

_____

_____

_____

_____

_____

FAMILY TRADITIONS AND CUSTOMS WE WISH TO PRESERVE

His:

_____

_____

_____

_____

_____

_____

_____

_____

_____

_____

_____

_____

Hers:

_____

_____

_____

_____

_____

_____

_____

_____

_____

_____

_____

_____

OUR STORY

SYMBOLS OF OUR LOVE

*Hearts understand myths
and legends . . . problems come when
the mind intervenes*
by Eleanor DiGiulio

From *Lotus Buds*
Salesian Institute of Graphic Arts
Madras, India 1969

Our favorite song:

_____

_____

_____

Our favorite flower:

_____

_____

_____

Our favorite saying:

_____

_____

_____

Our favorite movie:

_____

_____

_____

Our favorite activity together:

_____

_____

_____

_____

OUR FUTURE

Names we might give our children:

_____

_____

_____

_____

_____

What will we be doing in five years?

_____

_____

_____

_____

. . . ten years?

_____

_____

_____

_____

. . . twenty five years?

_____

_____

_____

_____

. . . fifty years?

_____

_____

_____

_____

OUR FUTURE

ON OUR FIFTH ANNIVERSARY

Events and memories of the first five years of our marriage

_____

_____

_____

_____

_____

_____

_____

_____

_____

_____

_____

_____

_____

_____

_____

_____

_____

_____

_____

_____

_____

_____

_____

_____

_____

_____

OUR FUTURE

ON OUR TENTH ANNIVERSARY

Events and memories of the first ten years of our marriage

_____

_____

_____

_____

_____

_____

_____

_____

_____

_____

_____

_____

_____

_____

_____

_____

_____

_____

_____

_____

_____

_____

_____

_____

_____

_____

_____

_____

_____

_____

_____

OUR FUTURE

ON OUR TWENTY-FIFTH ANNIVERSARY

Events and memories of the first twenty-five years of our marriage

_____

_____

_____

_____

_____

_____

_____

_____

_____

_____

_____

_____

_____

_____

_____

_____

_____

_____

_____

_____

_____

_____

_____

_____

_____

_____

_____

_____

_____